The Light of Advent

Reflections on Hope, Peace, Joy, Love and Christ

Emma Witmer

The Light of Advent

Reflections on Hope, Peace, Joy, Love and Christ

Emma Witmer

Emma Witmer
2021

First Printing: 2021

ISBN 978-1-008-93006-3

Published by Emma Witmer
www.thisonelife2give.wordpress.com

Distributed by Lulu

Cover photo by Angie Dempster
@angie_d_pics

To all those searching for hope, peace, joy and love this season, or any season of the year. May you find it, and may you find it in, with, and through Christ.

Contents

Hope

Dawn's Early Light

"Today in the town of David a Savior has been born to you; he is Christ the Lord."

Luke 2:11

Breaking of the early sun
Across the morning's horizon.
Dawn's early light
Warms the crisp, cool air,
Dew on the chilled ground,
A frost,
Not yet thawed by the morning's light.

Then, a moment.
The moment.
The moment when
Morning's sun
Crashes through the window,
Bringing light once more
To break up the
Long.
Dark.
Night.

Hope has come,
But people do not yet know,
What happened the night before,
While asleep in their beds,
Recuperating after a long day's work.
They arise not knowing
The world has changed.
Something has shifted,
Something has come
That will alter the way life is lived.

A new hope.
A new spark.
A new excitement.
Just as the sun pierces through
Early morning's dark,
So this Light will pierce through
The darkest heart,
The darkest circumstance,
The darkest outlook on life.

This hope brings change,
Brings renewal,
Brings a new day,
Brings love,
Peace,
Joy,
Eternal life.

This hope so small,
Grows.
Like a spark turned into flame.
Like the breaking of dawn's sunrise,
To the brightest light of the afternoon sun.
Shining bright into the hearts of all people.

Hope has come.
Do you feel it?
Do you sense it?
A little spark of hope,
In a little baby boy.

Looking Forward

"Therefore the Lord himself will give you a
sign: The virgin will be with child and will
give birth to a son, and will call him Immanuel.
He will eat curds and honey when he knows
enough to reject the wrong and choose the
right. But before the boy knows enough to
reject the wrong and choose the right, the land
of the two kings you dread will be laid waste."

Isaiah 7:14-16

Looking around,
Everything seems bleak.
Looking above,
Everything is cloudy and dark.
Looking back,
Everything is all destruction and sadness,
But looking ahead,
Looking forward,
Therein lies the hope,
The anticipation of things made new.

Where once there was no hope to be seen,
Now hope blossoms,
Hope springs up!

There will be a time
When things are not so bleak.
There will be a spark of hope
Stirring in people's hearts.
Men and women will smile again,
Children will laugh,
The sound of laughter will
Fill the space around you.
Hope has come,
Here to stay!
Hold on to it.
Don't miss it.
It is here.

A day is coming
When all things will be made right again.
Just open your eyes.
You'll see it.
Allow the light,
The hope,
To grow inside you.
Hold on to it,
And don't let it fade away.

You will once again see the day shine,
Shine so brightly in your heart,
In your life.
Don't give in now.
Hold on to hope.

Look forward,
And see it blossom.

Stars

"We saw his star in the east and have come to worship him."

Matthew 2:2

Sparkling high
In the midnight sky,
The sky so dark,
Foreboding if not for the twinkling lights,
Lights that light up the sky,
Light up the dark.
Darkness vanishes,
Shrinks away,
As the multitude of bright lights
Shines down on us.

These burning balls of fire,
So far away,
Yet seem to give what we need,
Unknowingly.
Shining brighter
When darkness is overwhelming,
All around.
Pointing the way,
Leading us onward

19

To dawn's new light,
To new hope,
To new comfort and joy.

Just look up,
Look up when all seems dark,
To see a multitude of stars,
Shining down on us,
Watching over us,
Guiding us,
Bringing light to our darkness.

Humanity's Hope

"'The days are coming,' declares the LORD,
'when I will raise up to David a righteous
Branch, a King who will reign wisely and do
what is just and right in the land. In his days
Judah will be saved and Israel will live in
safety. This is the name by which he will be
called: The LORD Our Righteousness.'"

Jeremiah 23:5-6

This drudgery,
This day in and day out,
This never-ending to and fro,
Of stress
And exhaustion,
Of trying so hard,
And coming up short.

When will it end?
When will a change come?
When can I breathe again,
Relax again,
Share common space again?

Memories of times past
Seem to fade,
Faster day by day.
Attention so focused on one thing,
One problem,
One disaster.
I scarcely remember
The old times,
The way it used to be,
When life seemed normal.

Now,
It's time to
Forget the past,
Move on,
Start anew,
Create a new normal.

But life does not feel normal now,
Not even if it's created anew.
Life has become
A gargantuan ball of steel wool,
Cold and painful to the touch.

Where is the hope?
Hope for a change,
Hope for an end to turmoil,
Hope for reconciliation,
Hope for a new tomorrow.

The only hope
Is unseen,
Dwelling deep within,
Some days deeper than others.
Hope that a new day comes,
A hope,
A faith,
A knowledge
That God is guiding me through.

A hope that is bright like the midday sun,
A hope that.
Though sometimes buried,
Rises again each day,
However small,
Never fading,
Never failing.
A hope placed,
In the One who holds me,
Who holds the world.

Hope

"He will not falter or be discouraged till he establishes justice on earth. In his law the islands will put their hope."

Isaiah 42:4

Not chance.
Not circumstance.
Not coincidence or crossed fingers
Or "que sera sera".

It is not fickle or fleeting,
But firm and forever-lasting.
Not unforeseen,
But long-expected and prophesied.

Hope.
Hope is alive.
It is living, vibrant and earth-shattering.
Hope is
Something so grand
Coming in such a tiny form.

Because our Father saw our lives
So dark and lost
And chose to come to the rescue,
We have hope.

Because Mary said, "Yes,"
We have hope.

Because God in Jesus came down to us,
We have hope.

Because Jesus grew and experienced life,
We have hope.

Because Jesus taught a better way to be,
To live,
To do,
We have hope.

Because Jesus came to make us new,
We have hope.

Because Jesus said, "Yes"
And walked a long, torturous road,
We have hope.

Because Jesus breathed his last,
And breathed his Life in us,
We have hope.

26

Because in this life you will have trouble,
But because Jesus overcame,
We have hope.

Hope in us,
Around us,
Before us,
Behind us.
Hope is here,
Because Jesus is here.

Peace

My Prince of Peace

"So Joseph also went up from the town of Nazareth in Galilee to Judea, to Bethlehem the town of David, because he belonged to the house and line of David. He went there to register with Mary, who was pledged to be married to him and was expecting a child. While they were there, the time came for the baby to be born, and she gave birth to her firstborn, a son. She wrapped him in cloths and placed him in a manger, because there was no room for them in the inn."

Luke 2:4-7

First, news that God has chosen me.
Rocking my world,
And in wonder,
I say yes.
I am God's servant.
I choose to honour him,
Every hour,
Every day,
For he is my God.

Then the angel says I will bear a son.
I have been with no one,
But I will become pregnant,
And give birth to a son,
Not just for me, but for all humankind.
I am shell-shocked.
I don't know how this can be,
But I am willing.
I am God's servant.

The weight of the pregnancy,
And the weight of what this means,
Wears me down.
My family, my friends,
They will all think I've sinned.
What can I do?
I must honour God and follow him.
He will provide a way,
Even when I'm not sure how.

Joseph, my beloved,
My betrothed,
Accepts me,
Accepts this child,
Saves me, and saves us,
From death,
From what the people have a right to do.
I will forever love and be grateful
For this man.

As time goes on,
And life becomes more uncomfortable,
We get news,
Not good news,
Not like the child I carry.
We must travel to Bethlehem.
The Romans order it,
So we must obey.
It will be a long, uncomfortable journey.
Why must we go?
Why at this time?
A week of travel, maybe more,
When my child is to come very soon,
Why, my God? Why now?

We go.
And we get there,
Just in time.
In Bethlehem, though unconventional,
We find a place.
I give birth to my first child,
My beloved names him Jesus.
What a wonder, what a sight.
God's son. My son.
What a miracle this child is,
My prince of peace,
To bring peace to the world.

We love him,
We enjoy him.
But all is not perfect.
Soon after, we must leave.
We are warned by God,
By his angel,
That we must leave,
Escape for our lives.
The king is furious,
Prepared to kill all young children,
So we must flee.
We must leave our home,
Our family,
Our friends.
When will this turmoil end?
When will my prince of peace,
Bring me peace,
Bring me rest,
Bring peace to the world?

My child,
My Lord,
My Jesus,
We need your peace,
Your Good News,
Your salvation,
For all.
Help us,
My prince of peace.

Not Here

"Praise be to the Lord, the God of Israel,
because he has come and has redeemed his
people. He has raised up a horn of salvation for
us in the house of his servant David."

Luke 1:68-69

Thoughts flood my mind
Of Christmases past,
Of time spent together,
Of joy and laughter.

I still hear your laughter,
Still see your smile,
Still feel your warm hugs,
Your gentle kisses upon my cheek.

This time of year,
With plans of family coming together,
Brings memories flooding back,
Joyous times with family,
Along with sad thoughts,
With the fact that
You are not here.

Christmas,
When family comes together,
When we turn our thoughts to others,
To good will,
Peace among us,
Love for our neighbour.
I remember now more than ever,
The love I had for you,
Still have for you,
Gone so suddenly.

Dearly missed,
Sad that you are not here,
But filled with joy and peace,
That you are with your beloved,
Lost so long ago,
And that you are with Jesus,
The one we celebrate this time of year,
Whose coming we praise God for.

He came,
As a little baby,
In the most innocent way,
Went through life as we do,
So we may relate to him,
Know him,
Praise him,
Accept him,

And be with him,
Just as you are now.

You are at peace.
For that, I thank God.
The Prince of Peace,
Who came to us so long ago,
Now greets you every day.
And so I am filled,
With hope,
With peace,
With joy.

Fear Not

"An angel of the Lord appeared to Joseph in a dream. 'Get up,' he said, 'take the child and his mother and escape to Egypt. Stay there until I tell you, for Herod is going to search for the child to kill him.'"

Matthew 2:13

Threat of danger,
Harm,
Pain.
This is fear.
How present it was in Roman times
When crucifixions were numerous,
Where death lurked around the corner
At the mere mention of the name of Christ.

Fear is real,
Causing real physiological responses:
A racing heart,
Sweaty palms,
Shaking hands,
Hyperventilation,
Panic attack.

Fear is real,
And if left
Unchecked,
Unnoticed,
It can cause anger to rise.

Joseph, taking his family and fleeing.
The threat from Rome - real.
The fear for his life,
And that of his new family -
Very real.
Leaving home,
The familiar,
Their own families,
The life they had built.
Anger - beginning to bubble up.

Did it take root?
Did he become angry at the situation,
At Herod,
At God,
At the work it took
Just to keep his family safe?

If it had,
How great was his suffering?
Did his anger lead to suffering?
Did he suffer more than needed

Because of his anger,
Because of his fear?
Did he let it get a hold of him,
Allowing fear to rule in his heart,
His mind,
His body?

Do I let fear rule in my being?
Do I let anger fester?
Do I suffer needlessly,
Or more than needed,
Because of my fear,
My anger?
Where do I make room for God?
God made room for Jesus,
When there seemed to be no room.
Can I make room for Jesus,
For his peace that passes understanding,
For his deep, abiding comfort,
To rule in my heart,
In the place of fear and anger?
Do I make room for him,
To trust him with my life,
With each situation?

Blessings and curses,
Peace and fear,
Joy and anger,
Comfort and suffering.

41

Which will I choose this day?
I choose,
I choose…

Good Will

"'Be strong, do not fear; your God will come,
he will come with vengeance; with divine
retribution he will come to save you.' Then will
the eyes of the blind be opened and the ears of
the deaf unstopped. Then will the lame leap like
a deer, and the mute tongue shout for joy."

Isaiah 35:4-6

Turmoil.
Anxiety.
Fear.
Worry.
Stress.
Insecurity.

All so real.
All so prevalent,
Becoming much stronger,
Day by day,
Feeling powerless over them,
Taking over my being,
Becoming who I am,
How people see me.

When will freedom come?
When will my mind see,
My eyes open,
My heart realize,
Freedom has already come.
Did I miss it?
Where did it go?
Did I not have it once?
How do I get it back?

Freedom from me,
Freedom from the churning in my heart,
Emotions running wild,
Life getting away from me.

It's on the horizon.
Will I see it?
There's a stirring in the air.
Will I feel it?
There is tranquility for the mind,
Calm for the heart,
Peace for the soul.
It is mine.
I can take it.

Jesus came, so I can have it.
He brought good will.
Good.
Will.

For everyone.
That includes me.
Includes you.
He came to bring peace.
To everyone.
Including you.
Including me.

But it's not what you expect.
It's nothing the world gives,
Offers,
Or understands.
This peace is so deep,
It is unfathomable,
It surpasses all understanding,
It takes root deep in your heart,
Your mind,
Your soul.

So be strong,
Do not fear.
Do not be anxious.
Do not worry.
Do not stress.
Open your heart,
Open your eyes,
Open your mind,
And allow this peace,
This amazing peace,

To take root,
To grow inside you,
And bring immense joy.

Peace

*"Glory to God in the highest, and on earth
peace to [those] on whom his favor rests."*

Luke 2:14

In a world where
Up is down,
Right is left,
North is south,
East is west.

A topsy turvy world,
With war and destruction at every turn,
Where there is such hatred,
May we be instruments of peace,
May we stand solid on the rock,
Who is the Prince of Peace.

In a place of confusion and chaos,
May the peace that
Passes all understanding
Abide in our hearts,
Abide in our minds.

In a world of busy,
Of running to and fro,
Of constantly on the go go go,
May we cling to Jesus,
Who offers a gift,
Nothing like the world can give,
A peace for our troubled and thirsty soul.

The best gift yet, in the tiniest package,
The only gift that gives to us,
Deep-abiding,
Soul-embracing,
Deep-sighing,
Peace.

Joy

What Joy

*"The people walking in darkness have seen a
great light; on those living in the land of the
shadow of death a light has dawned. You have
enlarged the nation and increased their joy,
they rejoice before you as people rejoice at the
harvest."*

Isaiah 9:2-3

News to share,
A joy to shout,
A celebration to be had.

What we have waited for,
Finally - arrived!
It seems so long,
Impatient we were,
And now we live to see this day,
This moment.
The time has come,
The time we waited for,
When our sorrows will
To joy be turned.

We will shout with joy!
We will dance with glee.
If yesterday we had been told,
Today would be the day,
We may not have believed,
For we never thought we would see
This day,
As real,
As true,
Coming true before us.

Our anguish was so deep,
The turmoil so real,
Our sight to any hope or joy was lost.
We were blind,
Unable to move,
Unable to believe what was said
So long ago.

But now we see.
We believe,
We celebrate,
We shout, "Oh joy of joys!"

The wrong that has been done,
It no longer matters.
Those who have cut us deep,
We no longer feel the pain.
We won't forget,

But now our hearts are fixed,
Set on the joy before us now.

The rebirth has come.
We are being reborn.
We are seeing hope.
We are seeing the promise come to light.
True light,
True love,
Given to us as a gift.
And we rejoice!

Light

"Where is the one who has been born king of the Jews? We saw his star in the east and have come to worship him."

Matthew 2:2

Even in the darkest night
We see - we are drawn to -
Light.

The flicker of a campfire,
The twinkling of lights
Strung up in the coldest season.
The beauty of a multi-coloured sunset.
The shine of the moon,
Reflecting off the water.
The Northern Star:
Brightest among thousands,
Guiding our way.

And the emotion these lights evoke,
Oh the emotions.
In the darkest mood,
In the saddest night,

In the murkiest confusion,
And the deepest depression,
These lights pull at our hearts,
And offer so much.

A flicker of hope.
A glimmer of joy.
A smile breaking through the frown.
The slightest sigh of relief.
Something to get us through,
Keep us going,
Enough to see us through to
The morning's light,
The dawn's fresh start.
As light is no longer a glimmer
But comes rushing in to help us through.

Lowly Shepherd

*"So [the shepherds] hurried off and found
Mary and Joseph, and the baby, who was lying
in the manger. When they had seen him, they
spread the word concerning what had been told
them about this child, and all who heard it were
amazed at what the shepherds said to them. But
Mary treasured up all these things and
pondered them in her heart. The shepherds
returned, glorifying and praising God for all
the things they had heard and seen, which were
just as they had been told."*

Luke 2:16-20

Is this real?
Could it be true?
Is what the angel said true?
I have to go and see for myself!

As fast as my feet would carry
An old man like me,
I hurried to see this new Messiah
That the angel declared has come.

I searched and searched.
Where could he be?
The Messiah must be somewhere special,
A place for a king,
But the angel said
He would be in a manger.

Finally, I see him,
In the lowest of places,
In a manger for a bed,
Wrapped in cloths.
What a sight I thought I would never see.
Someone like me, day after day,
Looking after sheep,
One of the first to see the newly come
Messiah,
The Saviour of the world.

Why me?
What have I done
To merit such an honour?
Nothing.
I have done nothing.
And maybe that's the truth of it.
Anyone, even a lowly shepherd,
Can come and rejoice,
Come and worship
This newborn king.
This miracle from heaven.

This prince who would bring peace.
The one who will bring
Comfort to the downtrodden,
Joy to those in the midst of sorrow,
Peace to the conflicted,
And love to the unseen of the world.

This child, this king,
Is for all the world.
What can I do but rejoice,
But sing praise,
But bring glory to this king.
Listen, everyone,
No matter who you are.
Listen, hear this!
A saviour is here.
He is here for you.
He loves you,
No matter who you are.
He will bring peace and joy to all.
Come and worship him,
For he is Christ, the Messiah,
The Saviour of the world!

Sing Glory

"Suddenly a great company of the heavenly host appeared with the angel, praising God and saying, 'Glory to God in the highest.'"

Luke 2:13-14

This is amazing,
Look what God is doing,
What he has done!

Taking a woman,
A woman on whom his favour rests,
Seeing her heart to serve God,
And serve him she did!

She said, "Yes,"
Glory to God.
She allowed God to choose her,
To carry his own child!

Now the world has hope anew.
The world will be able to see God anew.
The world will be able to accept
An amazing gift,

Not just of his one and only child,
But of salvation.

What an amazing thing this is,
Glory be to God!
And what amazing things
Are about to happen.
Miracles,
Mercies,
Forgiveness,
And salvation,
All wrapped
In a bundle of swaddling cloths.

The world has been waiting,
And if the world is watching,
It will see it happen,
Right before their eyes.
A glorious work,
All done out of love,
Unending love,
For all the world.
Glory to God!

Joy

"The Word became flesh and made his dwelling
among us. We have seen his glory, the glory of
the One and Only, who came from the Father,
full of grace and truth."

John 1:14

Abundant,
Exceeding,
Deep-rooted,
Unshakable,
Joy.

When all around is
Destruction,
War,
Poverty,
Hurt,
One thing is found so deeply rooted,
It cannot be shaken.

Joy.
Not happiness.
Not an emotion that comes and goes

With the passing of events.
Joy in the midst of hurt.
Joy in the midst of difficulty.
Joy in the midst of never-ending change.
Joy in the midst of sadness and grief.

A paradox.
Deep, sometimes hidden,
Truth.

Joy in his presence.
Joy in his never-ending,
Abiding-with-us love.
Joy in his salvation,
His salvation to us.
Joy of peace and love and hope and Christ.
All the things
Tied together in the one who
Came to live among us.
In the one who gave us grace
Wrapped in a baby.

And so we have
Abundant,
Exceeding,
Deep-rooted,
Unshakable,
Joy.

Love

Like a Father

"But after he had considered this, an angel of the Lord appeared to him in a dream and said, 'Joseph son of David, do not be afraid to take Mary home as your wife, because what is conceived in her is from the Holy Spirit. She will give birth to a son, and you are to give him the name Jesus, because he will save his people from their sins.' All this took place to fulfill what the Lord had said through the prophet: 'The virgin will be with child and will give birth to a son, and they will call him Immanuel' - which means, 'God with us.'"

Matthew 1:20-23

Here I was,
A humble man,
A hard-working man,
Working hard to marry
A woman I love dearly.
We were engaged.
She became pregnant.
What was I to do?
Everyone looked at me,

Wondering what I would do,
Would I cast the first stone?

I was making plans to divorce her,
But I was stopped.
An angel intervened - an angel!
How can you argue
With an angel sent by God?
The angel explained how
My beloved became pregnant.
An angel had appeared to her, too.
With all these angel-sightings,
This must be something big.

God was on the move,
God was at work.
My beloved was pregnant with God's son.
Wow!
The angel told me to name the child;
I was to be a parent to this child.
And not just any child
But God's child,
My beloved's child,
My child.
The child that is to be called,
"The God who saves is with us,"
Jesus is Emmanuel.
God incarnate.
Love incarnate.

I will listen.
I will choose love.
Just as God has done and shown.
I will be my beloved's.
I will raise this child as my own,
I will be a step-parent,
Be a father.
I will love the child as God has loved us.
And this Son will grow to love the world,
And save the world.

I will do as the angel has said.
I will name the child: Jesus.

What Matters Most

*"'Hear, O Israel, the Lord our God, the Lord is
one. Love the Lord your God with all your
heart and with all your soul and with all your
mind and with all your strength… Love your
neighbor as yourself.' There is no
commandment greater than these."*

Mark 12:29-31

What matters most,
Above all else,
Because of everything,
In spite of everything -
Love.
There is always love.

What doesn't matter?
Material things.
Your car,
Or the fact that you don't have one,
Your style,
Your new or tattered clothes,
Your job or education,
None of this matters.

What matters is love.
Loving yourself,
Loving your neighbour,
Loving the stranger
Walking down the street ahead of you.

Remembering those you once loved,
How much you loved them,
How much they loved you,
How you got excited every time
They smiled,
Came through the door.

Remembering the lives you touched,
And how they impacted you.
Remembering how much you gave,
And all they gave you.

Love and human connection,
That's paramount.
That's what we're made for.
That's what we're meant to do,
Above all else.

Love God.
Love others.
It's that simple.
Why do we complicate it?
If you don't love,

You're just making a racket,
Being loud and noisy, with no purpose,
Accomplishing nothing.
Without love.
Without connection,
We are nothing.
Empty shells.
Void of our true selves,
And all we're meant to be.
For we're meant to be love.
Tangible.
Real.
Love in action.

Love

*"For God so loved the world that he gave his
one and only Son…"*

John 3:16

Deep,
True,
Raw,
Radical,
Love.

Long-lasting,
Overflowing,
Valiant,
Extravagant,
Love.

High,
Deep,
Wide,
Long,
Amazing love.

Forever and always,
Tore into our existence,
Changed us forever.
Pulled on our heart strings,
Spoke so tenderly and deeply,
Speaking truth in Love so divine.

Magnificent,
From on high,
Flowing here below,
To God, from God,
And to others.

The radical love that moves so deeply,
Stops us in our tracks,
Utterly unconditional,
Incomprehensible,
Unfathomable,
Grace-filled,
Pure,
Love.

Love Abounds

*"What is man that you are mindful of him, the
son of man that you care for him?"*

Hebrews 2:6

From creation,
To present day,
Love flows deep,
Woven into the fabric of our being.

Yet.
Yet we look around,
And there is hate.
Where did we go wrong?
Where did we begin to put
Belief and opinion
Before relationship,
Before the inherent
Value and worth
Of another human being?
When?
Where?
How?

What gradual progression
Has caused our blindness?
What teaching
Over hundreds of years
Have we believed,
Have we accepted without question,
That has placed scales on our eyes,
Plugs in our ears,
Stones in our hearts?

Have we become so blind,
So deaf,
So hard-hearted,
That we cannot see the 'other' as human?
When did we start believing that
Not everyone has
Equal stature and dignity,
Simply because they are human?

Cries for help ignored.
Equity ungranted.
A simple right to breathe denied.
Missing and murdered and
Justice forgotten.
Where is the love?

In the single parent giving everything.
In the random act of kindness for the
stranger.

In the spouse who sacrifices,
Endlessly gives.
In the child who gives away their toys,
So an unknown child can have
Even. Just. One.

Love exists.
It is deeply rooted,
Ingrained in the human heart.
It was exemplified
In Christ.

Taking in tax collectors,
Prostitutes,
Adulterers,
Liars,
And so many more.
Showing them love,
Treating them as equals.
Humans.

Demonstrating a new way to live,
A new way to love,
So we can live in harmony and unity,
Under the love of God,
The same love
With which we were all created.
So let's choose love.
Love our friends,

Love our enemies,
So that we can see
Love abound.

All For Us

"For to us a child is born, to us a son is given, and the government will be on his shoulders. And he will be called Wonderful Counselor, Mighty God, Everlasting Father, Prince of Peace."

Isaiah 9:6

A gift for me,
Just for me?
What's the thought?
What's the reason?

Am I that special?
Am I that loved?
That worthy?
That valued or deserving?

Here's some truth - I'm not.
I'm really not.
I don't deserve anything.
Look at my life,
My actions,
My thoughts,

My heart.
I'm not worthy of a single thing.

Yet, the gift is still given.
Will I take it?
If I feel so unworthy,
It feels so wrong to take it.
But it comes with such love,
Such desire,
For peace,
And reconciliation,
To see unity once more,
So I graciously accept.

But first -
First I must open my hands,
Loose my grip,
Let love in,
Let the gift in.
I know it is good,
And good for me,
But, still so hard.

I strain,
I close my eyes,
Worried about what might happen,
If I actually open up,
Let go.

I release,
Open hands,
Sigh,
Breathe in,
Out,
Calm,
Peace,
Love coming in.

Almighty Counsellor,
Prince of Peace,
Everlasting God.
Owner of this gift everlasting,
Bringing peace,
Love,
To every heart,
Including mine.

Christk

Christ

Small Hands

"While they were there, the time came for the baby to be born, and she gave birth to her firstborn, a son."

Luke 2:6-7

Tiny child
With small hands, and small feet,
Born in the most lowly of places,
Unlikely,
Unseeming,
Unthinkable of places.

Innocent baby,
Child of God,
To grow like any other,
But become so much more.

Tiny face with wide eyes,
Taking in the world around you,
A world you created,
A world you would one day save.

Your small hands,
Now clinging to your mom,
Holding her for warmth,
Would one day reach out,
Stretch out,
Showing love to the world,
Doing miracles.
Healing hurts,
Raising the dead.

Rough hands,
A carpenter's hands,
With a soft, loving touch,
Showing a better way to live.
Beautiful hands, pointing the way,
Forgiving a multitude.

Blind see.
Deaf hear.
Lame walk.
With just a touch of your hands.

These now small hands,
Would grow to be
Stretched on a tree,
Pierced to save the world.
The small, innocent hands,
Would do so much.

Now we celebrate you,
And all the big things
Your small hands will do.

No Room

*"See, the former things have taken place, and
new things I declare; before they spring into
being I announce them to you."*

Isaiah 42:9

No room
Here at the inn.
No place for me,
For us.
Where is it that I might do this?
Where is it that I might find some comfort
In the midst of this unspeakable pain?
This pain that presses down on me,
The fear and anxiety of finding
No place for me,
No place for this child,
An added grief I bear.

No place.
Will there be a place in the hearts of people
For the Saviour that is to be born?
For this light
That will come into the world?

Will they find a place,
Will he find a way,
To provide a place in their hearts for him?

In their hearts,
The hearts of all humankind,
You will reach out with this light I carry.
You will bring their salvation,
The long-anticipated salvation,
The Messiah,
The Light of the world.
My pain means the wait is over.
You are coming.
You will open our hearts
To freedom once more.

Even if there is no place here,
There is room for you in this world,
In people's hearts,
In my heart.
Be with us and in us,
As you bring your light,
Ease our pain,
Bring us peace,
And your great love.

The Birthing Room

"Joseph son of David, do not be afraid to take Mary home as your wife, because what is conceived in her is from the Holy Spirit."

Matthew 1:20

Jesus was conceived in Mary's womb.
Then the time came.
The labour pains started
And grew stronger.
Deep breathing, and incredible pain.

Joseph by her side.
God within her.
Support by her side
As Mary went through deep pain.

Deep pain.
An experience of so many,
Coming in different shapes and sizes.

A hand to hold,
A heart to share.
An embrace to be felt.
A critical essential of true support.

Who will we allow into our birthing room?
Will we let our family,
A friend,
A professional
Know of our deep pain?
Will we reach out,
Grasp for a hand to hold,
To squeeze,
In our trying time,
In our pain,
To get us through,
Until we see new life being born?
Will we allow God into the birthing room,
Into our deep pain,
And allow him to carry us
Through the pain,
To support us,
Comfort us,
Give us strength,
Until new life is birthed through the pain?

Can we say,
"Come Jesus, hold my hand,"
As he works in our lives,
To bring his good work to completion?
Can we say yes?
Can I say yes?
Will we say yes?

Light of the World

"I am the light of the world. Whoever follows me will never walk in darkness, but will have the light of life."

John 8:12

When the world seems dark,
When hope seems lost,
When peace seems unattainable,
When love seems impossible,
When joy seems long-lost,
I am here.
I am the Light of the world.

No matter what the outside may look like,
No matter how dark,
No matter how confusing,
No matter how scary,
No matter how much all seems lost,
I am here.
I am the Light of the world.

Remember my promises.
Remember my good words.
Remember my ways of giving.

Remember my ways of thinking of others.
Remember my way of life.
I am here.
I am the Light of the world.

There will be understanding again.
There will be compassion
In the human heart again.
There will be kindness shown
To the Samaritan again.
There will be a bright sky shining again.
There will be a fresh breeze blowing in.
I am here.
I am the Light of the world.

I bring hope,
I bring peace,
I bring joy,
I bring love,
I am Christ.
I am here.
I am the Light of the world.

Good News Has Come

"And there were shepherds living out in the fields nearby, keeping watch over their flocks at night. An angel of the Lord appeared to them, and the glory of the Lord shone around them, and they were terrified. But the angel said to them, 'Do not be afraid. I bring you good news of great joy that will be for all the people. Today in the town of David a Savior has been born to you; he is Christ the Lord.'"

Luke 2:8-11

Good News has come,
Do not be afraid.
Good News has come,
Go see where he is laid.

Good News has come,
He will bring great joy.
Good News has come,
In just a little boy.

Good News has come,
In truth, he is now here.
Good News has come,

He will bring great cheer.

Good News is here,
For all people, all time.
Good News is here,
He is innocent, with no crime.

Good News is come,
Come, let the world hear.
Good News is come,
Come to cast away all fear.

Good News has come,
And one day he will hang on a tree.
The Good News that has come,
For you and for me.

Come rejoice, come believe.
Christ the Lord has come.
Come and praise him,
For one day he will say, "It is done."

Acknowledgements

A very special thank you to my family and friends who have supported me and my work. I appreciate you!

Thank you, especially, to my husband, Steve, who always continues to encourage me in my writing.

And a big thank you to all of you who are reading this book. Thank you for your support. I pray you find hope, peace, joy, love and Christ through these pages.

Printed in Great Britain
by Amazon